Stitch, Cloth, Shimmer & Shine

Dedication

To the ones who accept my little quirky ways, my creative chaos,
and to my friend, Christine.

Stitch, Cloth, Shimmer & Shine

Sarah Lawrence

SEARCH PRESS

First published in Great Britain 2012

Search Press Limited
Wellwood, North Farm Road,
Tunbridge Wells, Kent TN2 3DR

Text copyright © Sarah Lawrence 2012

Photographs by Paul Bricknell at Search Press Studios
Copyright © Search Press Ltd 2012

ISBN: 978-1-84448-627-4

Publisher's note
All the step-by-step photographs in this book feature
the author, Sarah Lawrence, demonstrating mixed
media craftwork. No models were harmed or asked to
get their hands dirty in the making of this book.

Sadly, Sarah Lawrence died before her book was published.
We have left everything exactly as she approved it. Many of you
reading this will know her as a feltmaker, embroiderer, author,
teacher, friend, or through her appearances on TV. However
you knew her, you will have known of her passion for her art,
her enthusiasm and her commitment to freely pass on her
knowledge and skills. We hope you will enjoy this book as
much as she enjoyed writing it, and take inspiration from her
work for many years to come.

Printed in Malaysia

Acknowledgements
Thanks to Tash and to Liz,
my 'friendly' crafty pal.

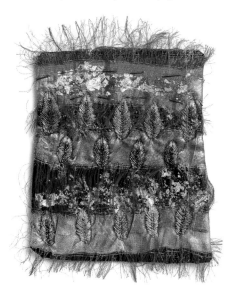

Contents

Introduction

The concept of this book is not for the reader to replicate all of the work, but to use the chapters as one would use a recipe book. Some things will excite and lead to many an hour of creative explorations. Others you will find are just the thing you want to add that 'something' to a piece you have struggled with (a little like adding a spice or garnish to enliven cooking). Then there are the store cupboard ingredients without which we cannot create our work.

Each section can be snipped and clipped with other sections to create a diverse range of combinations. The projects in the latter part of the book are explorations of these combinations and show the possibilities and opportunities the preceding chapters can offer.

I am often asked, 'Where do the ideas come from?' This can be a difficult one to answer. For the most part, the colours and layering of processes deliver a piece. I tend to look at the pattern of things rather than a landscape or portrait. I also keep collections of postcards and pictures that inspire me and I always keep a couple of sketchbooks on the go. Some of my sketchbooks are full of drawings, sketches and paintings, and take almost as much commitment as the textile work itself. Others, though, contain just a word, a scribble, a note to trigger my mind and allow me to explore pieces of work, some of which I know I will never have the time to make.

When asked for advice, I say: 'Be inquisitive about the media that you use and be disciplined in the usage'. Thinking about the many 'what ifs' before you really understand the fundamentals can lead to a lot of wasted time and a lot of unhappy or ugly work. You should enjoy what you create – life is too short to do things that aggravate the artist's soul. So try to understand the nature of the media you are using, and your creative work will flow from this familiarity.

The projects towards the end of this book show how the media and techniques described can be used to create vibrant, colourful pieces with plenty of shimmer and shine. All the methods shown have been used in my work over the years and nearly all have been enjoyed and explored by workshop participants, so they are tried and tested, like good recipes. I hope you find the contents of the book allow your creative juices to flow!

Opposite
Gold, Metal, Stitch
This piece uses the double-sided adhesive sheet method shown on page 14, and hand embossing shown on page 27 as well as colouring methods using alcohol inks (see page 34) and gilding waxes (page 38). Squares of double-sided adhesive sheet were gilded and machine stitched on to the black cotton background. Rectangles of metal were hand embossed, coloured and pierced and the holes were edged with little eyelets. The metal rectangles were then hand stitched into place. Completing the piece are four metal charm elements hand stitched into place. The edges were then sewn down and beaded (see page 68.)

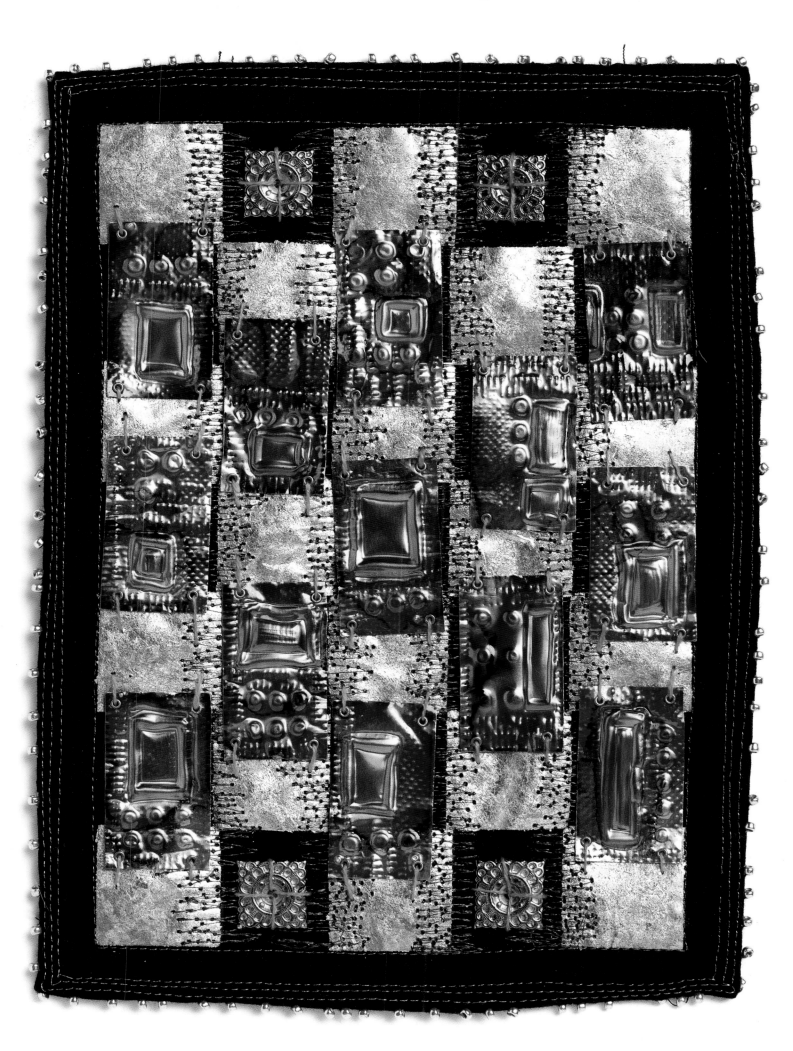

Using fabrics

Quite often it is the surface I use that helps the direction of the artwork. The colour, texture and malleability of the surface and its ability to absorb or reflect light all have a part to play in making an exciting surface that can be stitched and further enhanced.

I have been using all of the following methods to a greater or lesser degree over the years. Some will become favourites of yours, others may have to wait in the wings until they are needed to create just the effect you are looking for.

Shown below are the materials and tools you will need for the techniques in this chapter. If you cannot find them all, don't worry, part of the development of your own style is adaptation. Work with what you can find. For techniques throughout the book you will need a basic tool kit of scissors, rulers and something to protect your work surface from heat.

What you will need

Brown paper This is used to make my own fabric backgrounds. It can be acquired from packages you receive or from stationery or craft suppliers. I like a crisp feel as this generally indicates a good strong paper.

Wax crayons Used in the making of brown paper fabric. For better coverage and colour, use the best you can buy as opposed to cheap ones meant for children. These tend to have poor colour and wax content.

Metal leaf This consists of very fine sheets of metal foil, used for decoration. For craft applications, it is sometimes sold interleaved with backing sheets to make it easier to store and handle.

Craft ink spray These spray colours are available from a number of companies. Look for good mica levels and strong colours. Clean the heads out regularly to avoid blockages.

Gilding waxes These add colour and shine to projects. Avoid the ones made for furniture restoration as they may be very oily. Look for ones in little jars as opposed to metal tubes, as these are more suitable for use on textiles, paper and embellishments.

Interlining This is layered with items such as metal leaf or gilding flake, for its strength and translucency. It is available from haberdashery departments. Choose a lightweight one.

Gilding flake These extremely fine flakes of real or imitation metal are available in little pots and sometimes in flat packaging. Gilding flake comes in a variety of colours.

Inkpads These are usually used in rubber stamping, but here they are swept over your brown paper fabric to add colour.

Iron I use a small travel iron, but a normal sized one is fine. Be aware that you may contaminate the base plate when using it for craft purposes, so don't use it to iron clothes!

Making brown paper fabric

This is one of my creative textile store cupboard methods. We all have times when we just want to make something but we don't know what to use it for; well, brown paper fabric is what I often turn to at those moments. It is a surface that in itself will inspire. Also if you have a collection of these papers, you will always find a use for them because of their versatility.

1. Use good brown paper as this has a high rag content. Scribble over the surface with wax crayons in several different colours.

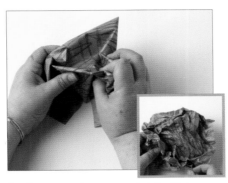

2. Screw up the paper tightly. This cracks the surface of the paper and makes it more like fabric. Flatten it out again.

3. Take an inkpad and sweep it over the crackled surface of the paper. The raised parts of the paper will pick up the ink.

4. Spray the brown paper fabric with red craft ink spray and leave it to dry thoroughly.

5. Take gold gilding wax and rub it over the surface of the brown paper fabric.

The finished brown paper fabric.

Layering interlining with metal leaf

When delicate and flimsy items are layered and laminated, they all bring their unique properties to the piece. With this composite creative surface, the strength and translucency are given by the interlining and the richness and luminosity are offered by the metal leaf. These particular surfaces can be stitched, printed, cut up and reassembled, or laminated with other fabrics.

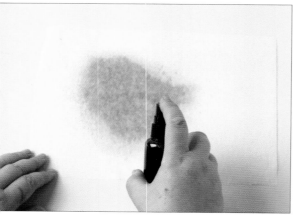

1. Spray iron-on interlining with turquoise craft ink spray. Allow to dry.

2. Take a square of coloured metal leaf and place it carefully on the sprayed interlining.

3. Fold the interlining over the metal leaf and iron the interlining, following the manufacturer's instructions.

The finished piece.

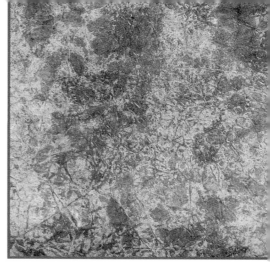

This row: three samples of brown paper fabric with embossing powders ironed on.

Interlining layered with metal leaf and sprayed with craft ink sprays.

Further ideas

Interlining layered with gilding flake.

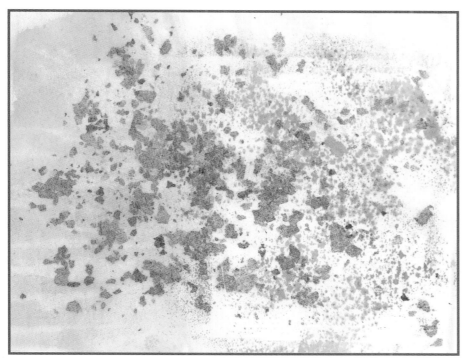

A piece showing interlining layered with gilding flake and sheer fabrics, with free machining (see pages 52–53).

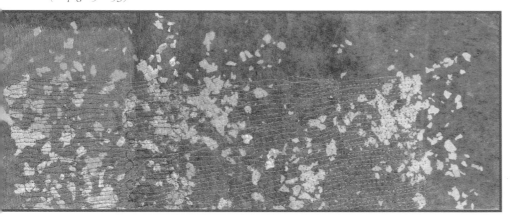

Gilding

There is foundation of richness that gilding techniques can give to creative textiles that is hard to beat. I have been using various gilding techniques in my work for more years than I care to say! I have always found the effect that the metal leaf and gilding flake offer to a piece of work visually enriching and exciting. The following methods are my favourites.

Although some of the items shown below may be unfamiliar to you, with the advent of the internet, you should have no problem finding suppliers. Alternatively, look on the Search Press website for details of stockists.

What you will need

Craft glue This should be a quick-drying, clear-drying, non-shrinking glue. Most PVA type glues are too wet and take too long to dry.

Glue stick Choose a glue stick that indicates it has super strength. This glue is likely to be less lumpy when you apply it and will deliver a more pleasing result.

Craft stickers These are available in a really diverse range of designs and finishes. They are available from all good craft outlets.

Stencils Use laser-cut stencils made from polyester film, as sometimes the cheaper die-cut plastic ones have a tendency to bend and crease.

Metal leaf and **gilding flake** are also used for these gilding techniques (see page 8). **Mica flakes** can be mixed in with gilding flake to give another texture.

Black cotton fabric I have used this as my background as it shows up bright colours and metallic elements so well. You could of course choose a different colour, but I strongly recommend that you use cotton.

Deckle-edged gilding

With this method you may need to practise a couple of times. The technique is one of those where you just have to work with the outcome. If you need to create a larger gilded area, keep adding the gilding flake in controllable sections. It is not advisable to try to do a very large area at one time. The background fabric needs to be a weave rather than something with a pile or a really fluffy structure. The colour is your choice. I have used predominately black or white fabrics throughout.

1. Take a piece of black cotton fabric and run a line of clear, quick-drying craft glue down it as shown.

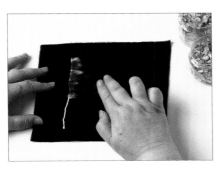

2. Smudge the line of glue outwards to the right with your fingers.

3. Sprinkle on gold gilding flake.

4. Rub off the excess gilding flake with the flat of your hand. The glue will have attached some of it as shown.

5. Make another line of glue to the right of the first one and repeat the sprinkling and rubbing off of the gilding flake to build up the effect.

The finished piece.

Using double-sided adhesive sheet

With this method, defined shapes can be added to your textiles. The adhesive sheet should not be too sticky. There are some with a red backing which are wonderful for paper crafting but if used for textiles, the adhesive is so sticky that you cannot easily draw a hand needle or indeed a machine needle through it. If appropriate materials are used, then stitching is not a problem. The adhesive sheet can be cut by hand or punched, or for more intricate shapes, there are die cutting systems available.

1. Peel off the backing from the double-sided adhesive sheet and stick it to a piece of black cotton fabric.

2. Peel the backing from a craft sticker and stick it half on and half off the adhesive sheet.

3. Sprinkle on Autumn Rose gilding flake.

4. Brush off the excess gilding flake. Continue sprinkling on more gilding flake and rubbing off the excess in this way until you have covered the adhesive sheet.

The finished piece.

Further ideas

Deckle-edged gilding overlain with
sheer fabrics and stitching.

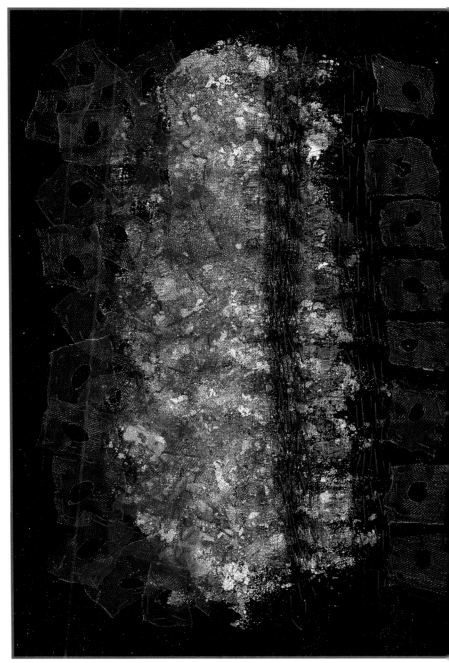

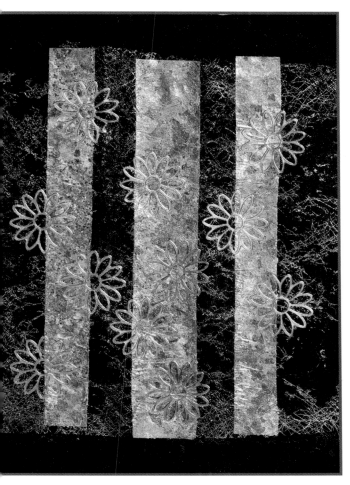

Stripes of double-sided adhesive sheet used with gossamer
webbing and craft stickers.

Double-sided adhesive sheet
combined with deckle-edged gilding
and a heart design.

Using glue stick with a stencil

As with the previous method, the use of stencils, whether professionally made or hand-cut from a sheet of plastic, allows more control over the design and placement. You will also notice that more than one colour or tone of gilding flake can be used, so there are many possibilities of graduating your gilding flake or even mixing your own blend.

1. Place a plastic crafting stencil on black cotton fabric and go over it with a glue stick. Make vertical movements of the glue stick to avoid undercutting the stencil and turn the stick as required. Apply glue over the outer edges of the stencil as well.

2. Lift up the stencil to reveal the glued pattern.

3. Sprinkle on silver, then variegated gold gilding flake, then leave the glue to dry.

4. Sweep off the excess gilding flake with your fingers.

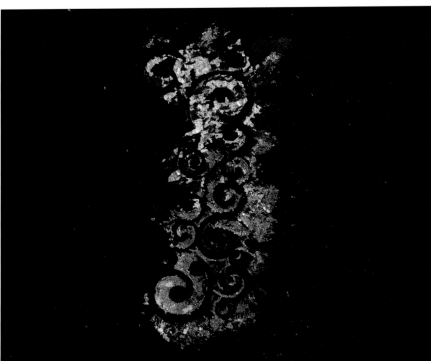

The finished piece.

A glue stick and stencil used with a deckle-edged gilding and stitching.

Further ideas

A glue stick used with a stencil, and the stencil then used with fabric paints to overcolour.

A glue stick and stencil used with foiling and solvent markers to overcolour the silver.

Using mica

Mica is a natural layered mineral which is found in many places around the world. It is generally available in irregular sheets but also in a number of pre-cut shapes ranging from circles to squares. As it is a naturally occurring material, there are wonderful variations. Some pieces are very clear; others have marks within the structure giving the impression of big cat markings. Mica adds a shimmer to any textile, with a natural honey toned glow, and it is marvellous because it can also be coloured.

What you will need

Mouse mat I use this instead of a specially bought piercing mat. Choose a soft-faced mouse mat so that you can pierce through the mica more easily. Alternatively a piece of dense foam could be used.

Piercing tool These are sometimes called poking tools or stilettos. They have a really strong pointed steel tip with a wooden handle. I use a fine-tipped tool for piercing mica.

Mica This is available in several grades, in sheets and also in pre-made shapes.

Scissors Use sharp, firm, strong scissors. If you use scissors that are not strong enough, you will not be able to cut the mica sheets easily.

Splitting

Sheets of mica are really easy to split into separate layers using just your thumbnail.

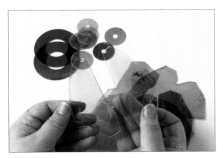

1. Insert your thumbnail between two layers in the sheet of mica.

2. Use your thumbnail to lever the layers of mica apart.

Cutting

Mica is also easy to cut into whichever shape you require. The ring-shaped pieces in the photograph are produced ready-cut for industrial uses but are also ideal for crafts.

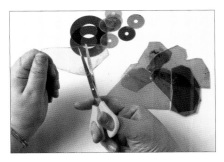

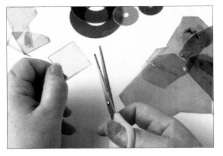

Cut mica using ordinary scissors.

The mica can be cut neatly to shape as shown.

Piercing

Mica can also be pierced, either to decorate it or to aid its attachment.

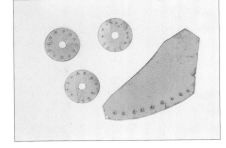

Below left: gilded and coloured mica squares with deckle-edged gilding and double-sided adhesive. Middle: pierced, coloured, stitched and beaded mica. Right: gilded mica with hot dots, fly stitch and straight stitch.

Place the mica pieces on a mouse mat and use a piercing tool to pierce holes as required.

The pierced pieces of mica.

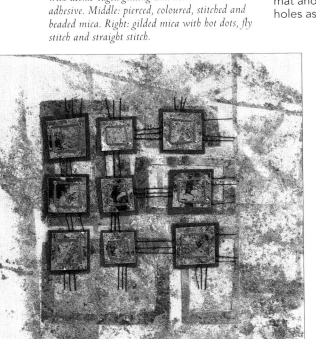

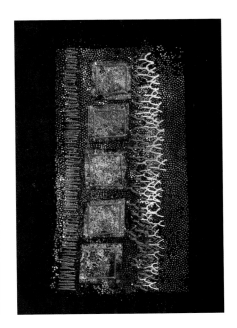

Using hot fusing adhesives

I will issue a warning with this way of working: it is addictive! This is another of my creative store cupboard techniques. It is a way of playing with the juxtaposition of shapes, colours and shine and it gives you the excitement of combining these to make a piece which can then be stitched, embellished and further enriched.

What you will need

Foils Use quality craft transfer foils. They tend to be available in 30.5cm (12in) squares. Check that foils are suitable for transferring on to fabric with an iron (some only transfer with glue and other types require heat press machines).

Fusible adhesives These are man-made fibres which melt when heated, so that when placed between fabrics, or between fabric and other materials, and then heated, they act as an adhesive. The range available nowadays is quite wide. **Fusible web** is protected by a removable backing sheet. **Gossamer webbing** (shown in black and white) is dry to the touch and fuses materials in a fine web design. Others that are available have a chevron design (see the piece at the bottom of page 65). **Hot dots** are tiny dots of heat bondable adhesive. You can mix the types of fusible adhesive used within projects.

Fabric paint Choose a range of textile paints that are heat fixed with an iron and do not have a really heavy consistency. A paint range that has a creamy consistency will be easier to use and thin with water. You will also need a mixing palette and brushes or sponge brushes to apply the paint. A packet of moist wipes is useful to have to hand. Clean brushes, sponges and palettes quickly after use.

Silicone paper This is used as a barrier between the iron and the project you are ironing. It is non-stick and will last for ages.

Metal leaf and **gilding flake** are also used for these techniques (see page 8).

Using fusible web

Have fun with this free way of layering. You will come to realise as this method becomes more familiar to you that you can trap threads, gilding flake and elements such as skeleton leaves between the adhesive fragments.

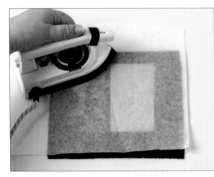

1. Paint pieces of fusible web in different coloured shiny fabric paints. Water the paint down to one part water to two parts paint to facilitate easier removal from the backing sheet. The better the quality of paint the more it can be diluted. Allow the paint to dry. Pull torn pieces of fusible web off the backing and place them on black cotton fabric.

2. Stick a rectangle of fusible web to the black fabric as shown, then cover the piece with silicone paper and iron on all the fusible web.

3. Peel the backing off the fusible web rectangle and place a sheet of chemically treated metal leaf on top. Place silicone paper on top and iron again.

4. Pull the edge of the metal leaf where it is not adhered to the fusible web.

5. You can save the pieces that come off between the sheets of a book of metal leaf.

The finished piece.

Using gossamer webbing

Gossamer webbing has generally been used for quilting and appliqué. The fine trails of heat-bonded adhesive webbing are magical when foiled and applied in combination with coloured surfaces. They are easily layered for more dramatic depth of tone, and of course they make a lovely surface to layer with stitches so that only a hint of a glint pops through.

1. Place the gossamer webbing on to black cotton fabric and place two different foils on top as shown. Place a sheet of silicone paper over the piece and iron it to activate the gossamer webbing.

2. Peel off the foils to show how much has stuck to the gossamer webbing.

3. The foil tends to stick over the gaps in the gossamer webbing, so scrunch, manipulate and rub the piece to take off the excess.

The finished piece.

4. Open out the piece again.

*Painted fusible web with added
heat resistant spangles.*

*Right: painted fusible web with netted adhesive
and heat resistant spangles. Below: gossamer
webbing used on a painted background.*

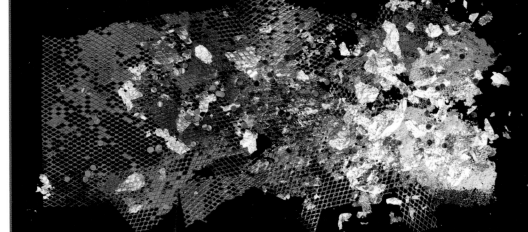

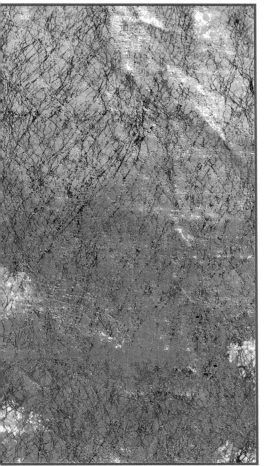

*Gossamer webbing and foil
used on brown paper fabric.*

23

Using hot dots

Using the heat-activated adhesive dots gives any surface that can be 'dotted' a very contemporary feel. Two sizes of dots are available. They can be combined or layered, and the paper backing sheet can be cut with scissors or die-cut for more intricate shapes. Use them in bold swathes, or just to highlight a small area. Stitch over them to create intriguing fractured light-reflecting patches. Paint over dotted areas, allowing the light-reflective foils to glow through the paint.

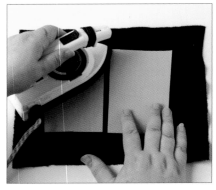

1. Place two rectangular pieces of brown paper-backed hot dots sheet face down on black cotton fabric and iron the backs to attach the glue dots.

2. Peel of the paper backing.

3. Place copper and silver-coloured foil over the hot dots and put a sheet of silicone paper over the top.

4. Iron to attach the foils.

5. Peel off the foils to reveal the effect.

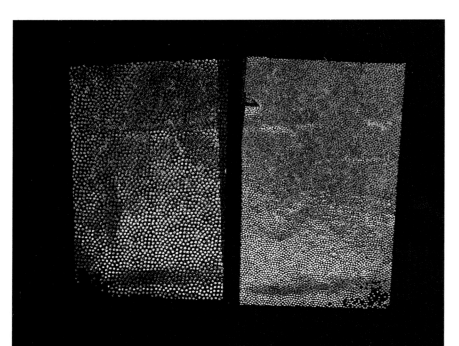

The finished piece.

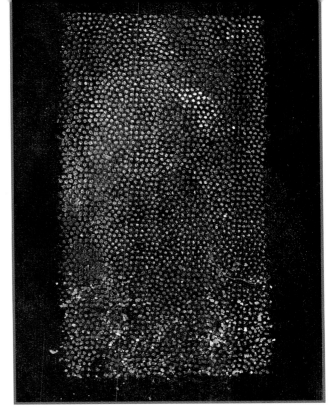

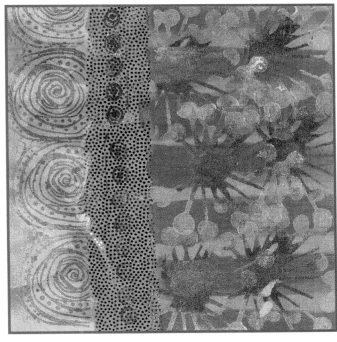

F u r t h e r   i d e a s

Left: hot dots used on blue velvet; above: on a printed and stamped piece.

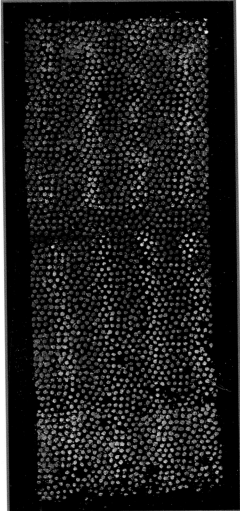

Far left: hot dots used with stitching and left: with coloured foils.

Metal manipulation

Metal has been added to textiles for adornment, protection, or as an indication of opulence for many centuries. The methods that I share here are easy to recreate and with practice you will get to know your metals sheets and the many possibilities they offer. Crafting metals are available in different finishes, and in gold, copper-toned and a variety of colours. The metals you choose should be thin enough to stitch and easily manipulated. Sometimes you may see metal sheet referred to as a shim. This is a term used for thin metals and these are appropriate for the techniques that follow.

What you will need

Craft metals These are available in a variety of finishes : gold, copper and various colours. The metal should be thin enough to bend easily and to pierce through with a needle.

Embossing tools Choose ball-ended tools: perhaps a small and slightly larger size as basics, and add to your selection when you find tools you like. A **nylon shaping tool** is used to dome circles of metal (see page 30). Old ballpoint pens and metal knitting needles also make very satisfying mark-making tools.

Texturing wheels These are used to pattern metal. The pattern appears as you roll the tool over it. Both embossing tools and texturing wheels are used with a **mouse mat**.

Craft punches Use medium to large paper punches. I also used a 3mm (1/8in) hole punch to create suitable holes for stitching metal pieces in place.

Die cutting machine This is used for machine embossing metal pieces. The metal is placed in a patterned embossing folder which is then fed through the machine. I would recommend a machine that has a 15.2cm (6in) tray, as this is likely to take all types of cutting dies and embossing folders.

Sewing machine This is used with the free machining technique to decorate metal circles and attach them to felt backing before doming (see page 30). As long as you have a straight stitch and a swing or zigzag capability on your sewing machine, you will be fine. You may wish to change your needle, but I have used a size 80 for all the samples and projects. Some may prefer a size 90 or even heavier needle for sewing metal, but if the metal is soft enough, you should not need a heavier needle. You may find that with a lot of use the needle point is dulled.

Scissors These are used to cut the felt backing for metal circles used in the doming technique.

Hand embossing

If you are confident, you can start to make your marks freehand. Alternatively, it is possible to draw on the metal with a solvent-based marker pen, draw the lines and marks with your tools and then when you have finished, wipe away the tracing marks with a solvent cleaner on a soft cloth or cotton wool.

1. Place your metal sheet on a mouse mat and firmly draw a wavy line with the large end of the ball tool.

2. Flip the metal over and go over the edge of the wavy line with the small end of the ball tool.

3. Use the large ball tool to push a line of dots into the metal. Flip the metal over again and push another line of dots next to the first, but on the other side.

4. Go round the edges of the dots with the small ball tool to define them.

5. Make a line to the right of the dots with a texturing wheel. Repeat.

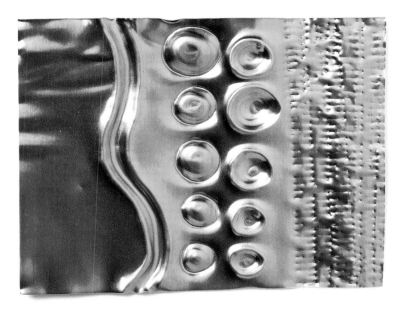

The finished piece.

Machine embossing

With the availability of personal die cutting and embossing machines, the world of surface manipulation has opened up for the creative textile enthusiast.
If you don't have one, I am sure that you will know a paper-based card crafter friend who has, so ask if you can play with it! I know that some groups have larger tools and machines that are loaned to group members.

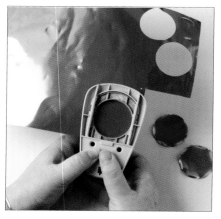

1. Punch out large circles from a sheet of metal with a craft punch.

2. Place them in the patterned embossing folder of your choice, ready to put through the die cutting machine.

3. Put the circles through the die cutting machine, following the manufacturer's instructions.

4. Take the circles from the patterned folder to reveal the embossed pattern.

5. Use a 3mm (⅛in) hole punch to make four holes around the edge of the circle.

The finished pieces.

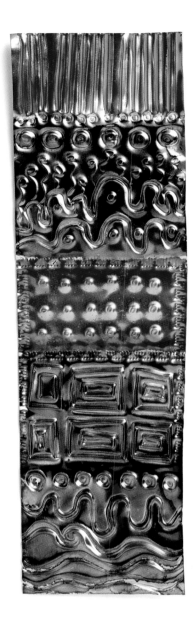

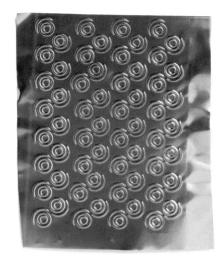

A machine embossed pattern.

Far left and left: hand embossed painted pieces.

Further ideas

Far left and left: painted machine embossed pieces.

Doming

The three-dimensional aspect of this very pleasing method of metal forming can add a sculptural feel to your artwork. When the metal begins to react to the movement of the shaping tool, the transformation is quite remarkable. Once it is shaped, however, it is very difficult to make it flat again, because the manipulation stretches the metal. With a little practice, the domed shapes can be worked so that they are really smooth.

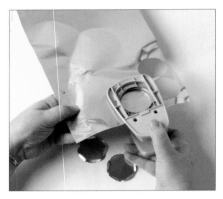

1. Punch out three circles of metal with a craft punch.

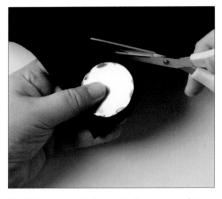

2. Take one circle and draw round it on black felt. Cut out the felt circle. Repeat for the other two circles.

3. Set up any basic sewing machine for free machining. Thread up with 912 King Tut variegated cotton thread. Stitch from the edge a little way into the circle and out again, then repeat, working round the circle.

4. Free machine all three circles in the same way. To begin creating the domed shape, start with the smaller end of the ball tool and rub with a circular motion in the middle of one of the circles.

5. Change to the nylon shaping tool and continue, circling outwards towards the edge of the circle. Repeat for one of the other circles.

6. Take the third circle and turn it over to the black side. Dome this circle in the same way. You will find that it is more difficult this time because you are working against the tension of the fabric.

The finished domed pieces.

A selection of domed pieces.

Further ideas

Above and left: Domed metal shapes added to printed and stitched metal sheet. Shapes can be stitched or glued in place. In the piece on the left, the metal has been coloured with solvent markers.

Colouring

As we progress with the different techniques, the question of colouring needs to be addressed. It is a creative delight to change the colour of things you have made. Colour can affect mood and the relationship of one material to another and of course we all have our favourite palette of colours. I have no problem with students working with the same colours if they bring them joy. There are purple people, earth-tone aficionados and green friends – so find your colour and work with it! However, a deeper understanding of colour mixing and the emotional connection colour can impart will help your work to truly reflect your artistic vision. It is tremendous fun to play with different colouring mediums to see what they offer. Then you have the choice of how you apply the colour: brushes, finger tips, sponges, print blocks or stamps can all be used.

What you will need

Alcohol inks These are solvent/alcohol based colouring fluids that are available in a variety of rich, transparent colours. They are ideal for colouring non-absorbent surfaces, and I have used them on mica, metal leaf and metal. The colours can be layered over each other. Use the appropriate clean-up fluids to remove colour or clean up after use.

Felt stamping tools These are felt patches with a wooden handle. The felt patches can be replaced. I use them to apply alcohol inks.

Solvent markers These pens dry quickly, and the solvent-based pigments will colour many non-absorbent surfaces, which is why they are so useful to the creative textiler. I prefer the brush-tip type as they are easier to manoeuvre and make more sensitive marks. I have used them here to colour metal leaf, metal, hooks and eyes, embossed metal and craft stickers.

Gilding waxes (see page 8). These are used to colour metal, charms, friendly plastic embellishments and brown paper fabric.

Fabric paints (see page 20). I have used these with **stencils** (see page 12). They can be applied with **dense foam stamps**. These are made from dense foam with a sponge top, which is cut to size to make an ideal applicator for paint as well as several other colouring mediums. I have also used **rubber stamps** with fabric paints, both to apply a pattern and to lift out a pattern from an area of paint.

Alcohol inks

Alcohol inks will give metal and other non-absorbent surfaces a distinct veil of translucent colour. There are enough colours available to suit all tastes. They are generally available in small plastic bottle with slim nozzles that deliver the amount of colourant you require. They can be mixed, but you need to work swiftly with them, as by their nature they set quickly. If you do something that does not please you, it can be removed with alcohol ink clean-up solution.

On mica

1. Place pieces of mica on scrap paper. Apply green and aqua alcohol inks to a felt stamping tool.

2. Stamp on to pieces of mica.

The coloured pieces of mica.

On metal leaf

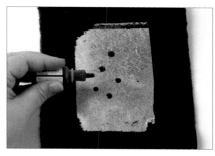

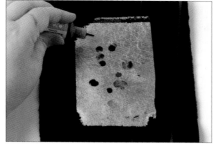

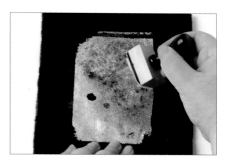

1. Drop deep red alcohol ink directly on to the metal leaf (mine was previously attached to black cotton fabric using fusible web).

2. Drop green alcohol ink on in the same way.

3. Add a third colour, blue, and use a felt stamping tool to move the colours around.

The coloured metal leaf.

On embossed metal

1. Pour yellow alcohol ink on to the embossed metal, allowing it to collect in the channels.

2. Apply red alcohol ink in the same way.

3. Pour on aqua alcohol ink, going over some of the other colours.

The coloured embossed metal.

Alcohol inks used on gilding flake adhered using double-sided adhesive sheet.

F u r t h e r   i d e a s

Alcohol inks used on machine-embossed metal.

Solvent markers

There are several makes of solvent marker. In essence they are the same, but the tips vary. I prefer the brush-tip type as opposed to the sturdy bullet-tip type, as the brush allows me to make more sensitive marks and to wriggle colour into nooks and crannies. The colour can be removed with appropriate solvent removers. The better quality pens will deliver a richer and more long-lasting colour. Darker colours show up better, but if a subtle tone is required, the lighter colours are perfect. I would advise a practice piece so you can assess the suitability of the colour range for your work.

On metal leaf

1. I used a pink solvent marker to go round the border of this heart design made from metal leaf, then I coloured parts of the central heart in the same way.

2. I used the same marker to blend the border into the gold leaf in the centre of the design.

The finished piece.

On metal

You can use a red solvent marker to add a spectacular finishing touch to your domed metal pieces.

The finished piece.

On hooks and eyes

Here, a purple solvent marker is being used to colour linked hooks and eyes.

The coloured hooks and eyes.

On embossed metal

1. Here I used a red solvent market in the channels made by hand embossing metal.

2. I then added brown solvent marker, and finally Prussian blue in the channels.

On craft stickers

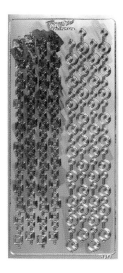

The craft stickers shown left have been coloured with solvent markers while on the sheet, then removed and applied to the finished piece, above.

Solvent markers were used on metal leaf in this stitched finished piece.

Craft stickers coloured with solvent markers were used on blue velvet.

Gilding waxes

Items with a texture can be enriched with gilding waxes to give a sophisticated enrichment of tone or colour enhancement. Good quality gilding waxes can be used on a range of surfaces including metals, fabrics and papers. The quality of the wax will be reflected in the way the wax will pick up detailing on the most subtle surfaces. Gilding waxes will often bring out hidden textures.

On metal

Here, cerise gilding wax is being rubbed into hand embossed metal.

On charms

Rubbing gold gilding wax into an intricate textured charm.

The finished charms.

On friendly plastic

Gilding wax being applied to stamped friendly plastic.

The finished piece.

On brown paper fabric

Aqua gilding wax being rubbed into the surface of brown paper fabric – a technique known as over-gleaming.

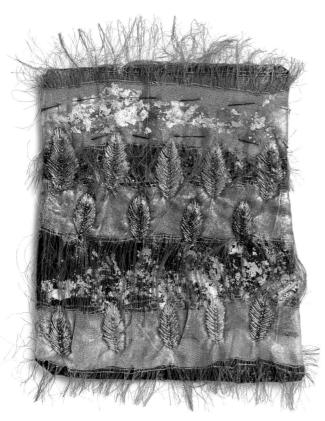

Gilding wax has been applied to the fly stitch decoration in this piece.

Gilding wax was used to add a shine to these stamped friendly plastic squares. The fabric has been printed with the same stamp.

Gilding wax applied to pieces made from friendly plastic.

Fabric paints

There is a plethora of fabric paints available; some are thin and watery and others are quite heavy and leave a plastic-like finish. Some are matt and some are very metallic. I suggest you choose a paint with a light, creamy consistency, which will dilute without losing colour potency, and will fix (if required) to your fabric with an iron. I also like a textile paint to have a little shimmer. This adds light and life to a piece of work. I am lucky enough to have my paints manufactured for me, but you should choose what works for you.

Using a stencil

Here, fabric paints are used through a stencil on top of foiled gossamer webbing.

1. I have used a craft sheet as a palette. Apply purple fabric paint to a dense foam stamp and take off the excess on the palette. Stamp through the plastic craft stencil in places.

2. Change to a new dense foam stamp to apply the second colour: blue.

3. Carefully lift the stencil to reveal the result.

The stencilled piece.

Using dense foam stamps

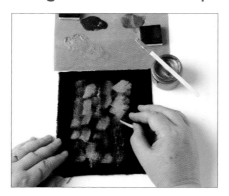

Here I used a dense foam stamp to apply copper coloured fabric paint to black cotton fabric, dabbing on the colour with random strokes.

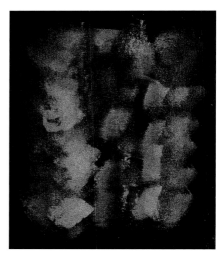

The finished effect.

40

Rubber stamping

1. Apply peacock fabric paint to a large rubber stamp (this one is on an acrylic block). Stamp on to black cotton fabric, then reapply the paint to the stamp and stamp again.

2. Lift the stamp to reveal the design.

The finished effect.

Rubber stamping to lift off paint

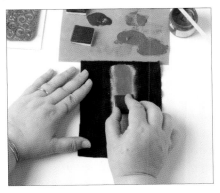

1. Use a dense foam stamp to stamp a line of copper-coloured fabric paint on to black cotton fabric. Leave the band of solid colour to dry.

2. Use another dense foam stamp to stamp peacock-coloured fabric paint over the top of the copper.

3. Apply the peacock paint to a large rubber stamp (this one is on an acrylic block).

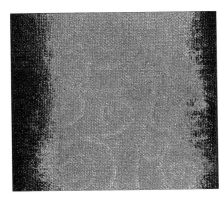

4. Apply the painted stamp to the wet peacock paint.

5. The stamp has the effect of lifting off paint.

The finished effect.

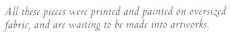

All these pieces were printed and painted on oversized fabric, and are waiting to be made into artworks.

Gold and bubblegum pink paint have been used with a stencil and with a dense foam stamp, and with rubber stamping and lifting off techniques.

Deckle-edged gilding (see page 13) on a purple cotton background was over-coloured with a square stencil and pink and copper fabric paint.

A black cotton background was randomly dabbed with paint using a brush and sponge. This was allowed to dry, then paint was applied using a spiral stamp.

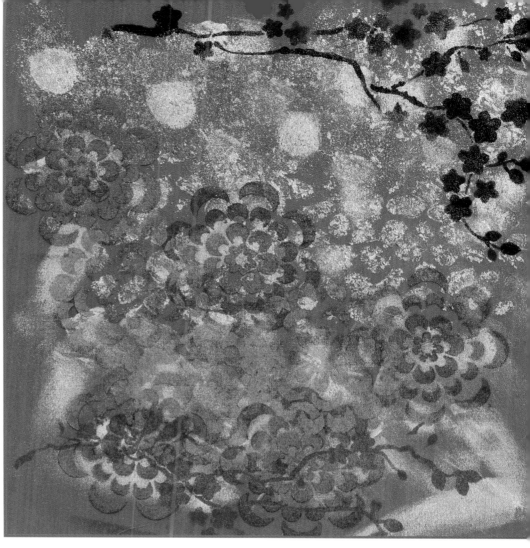

A background freely dabbed with rose and peacock paint colours was then over-stencilled with a floral stencil and gold paint.

A background created by deckle-edged gilding (see page 13) was over-stencilled with a chrysanthemum and cherry blossom inspired stencil.

Further ideas

Stitching

As you progress through the techniques, the urge to add some stitchery may well be starting to stir. Regardless of your skill level, the pleasure of making the lines of thread dance their way into lovely patterns with the aid of a needle is very appealing. Throughout history, people have stitched to decorate, strengthen and join fabrics, using needles made from whittled down wood and even pierced fish ribs. Now we can stitch with a sewing machine and combine that with hand stitching. Think about stitch size, thread weight, layering, squeezing and stretching the stitches, and use shiny or textured threads, or ply thin threads to make thicker threads – the possibilities are truly captivating.

What you will need

Cotton threads You need good quality cotton threads for hand and machine stitching, in a variety of colours.

Hand sewing needles Always use the right needle for the job. I use a selection of embroidery needles. These have long eyes and range in size to accommodate most hand stitching threads. Mostly I use size 7 needles. For really chunky threads, I use a crewel work needle, as they have a long, oversized eye and a sharp point, allowing you to 'punch' through fabric.

Cotton fabric You need a variety of colours, although I have used a lot of black to set off the bright colours and shiny materials I use. Have a spare piece of fabric to act as a scribble pad so that you can practise your stitching before you commit to your artwork.

Sewing machine You need one with a drop feed and a free motion or free machine foot. Make sure you read the manual, and have the machine serviced regularly.

Felt Black felt is used to back the fabric for the distortion technique shown on page 54.

Flower stitcher foot This is a special sewing machine foot used for the technique shown on page 56. It is a universal foot and will fit most low shank machines (the shank is the bit the feet fit on). It will not fit a machine with an integrated walking foot. If you have a high shank machine, you may have the necessary converter in your tools; if not, you will need to acquire one. Some machine companies produce their own version of the flower stitcher foot.

Hand stitching

Some of these stitch patterns will be very familiar; other may be quite new. Well-used stitches may become over-familiar. If you revisit them with fresh eyes and rework them on new backgrounds, they will work their way back to the forefront of your stitching repertoire. The rhythm of the movement of creating a handmade stitch should be part of its appeal. If it feels awkward to stitch, try to evaluate why that is. Is the thread too thick to pull through the background? One of the most common things I come across is too much thread. Only use a piece the length of your forearm, as refreshing the thread regularly makes the stitches look more evenly textured, and your arms will not ache as you draw the thread through the fabric.

Running stitch

Simply adjusting the way you insert the needle into your fabric will have an effect on the shape of the stitch. Gathering fabric on to the needle before you draw the thread through will give a pleated texture to the stitched area. Being disciplined in placing the needle vertically through the fabric and then pulling vertically through from the back will allow the stitch created to sit pertly on the surface.

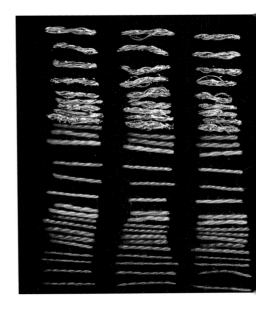

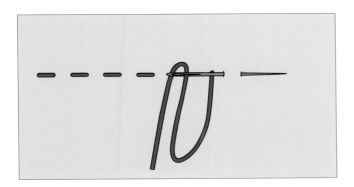

Running stitch diagram.

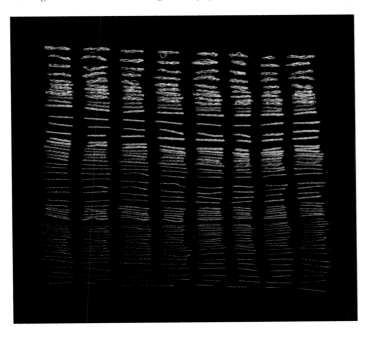

Running stitch worked in rows using a variety of threads.

Running stitch in subtle colours on a painted and sprayed background.

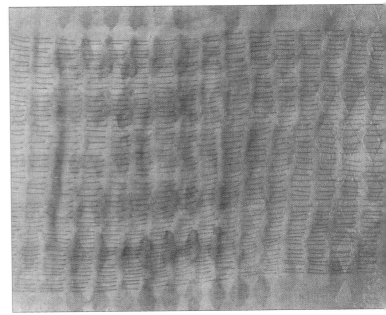

Fly stitch

This stitch is a true favourite of mine because it can be used singly or in pattern clusters, and it can be stitched to make dense, solid motifs. It works well with thick as well as fine threads and can be given different proportions.

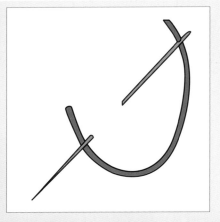

Step 1

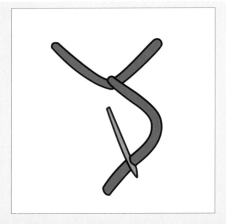

Step 2

Worked examples of fly stitch.

Fly stitch worked on black fabric.

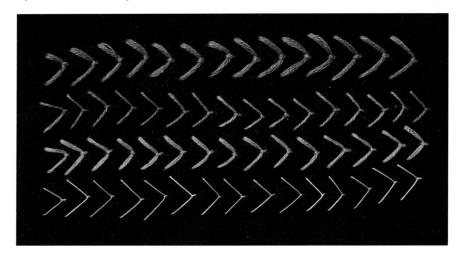

Fly stitch on a gilded piece.

46

Lock stitch

This stitch can be interlaced with a variety of fancy threads, as the interlacing is wound around the foundation of straight stitches. I like the little spaces which are good for introducing beads, creating even greater decorative possibilities.

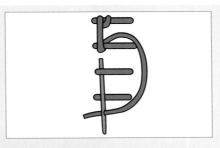

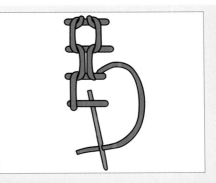

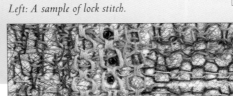

Left: A sample of lock stitch.

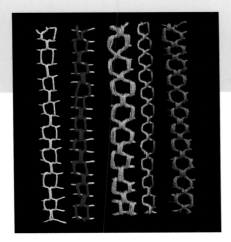

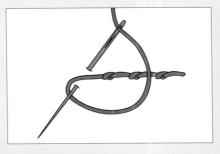

Lock stitch worked on a foiled gossamer webbing background.

Coral stitch

This is a linear stitch which can really add a lyrical element to the surface. It is easily manipulated to follow even complicated shapes and lines. It adds texture without being overpowering and although I prefer to use a smooth thread when stitching out coral, it does work well with bulkier threads and an appropriately chosen needle.

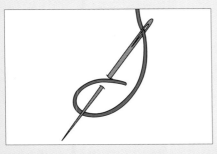

Step 1

Step 2

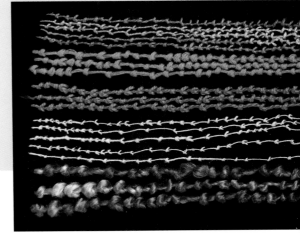

A sample of coral stitch in various colours and types of thread.

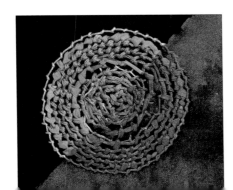

A coral stitch circle partially over-painted with fabric paint.

Couching

Thick threads, thin threads, difficult to stitch threads – these can all be used with this trapping stitch. The density of stitches and the direction in which they are placed will have an effect on the decorative effect of this surface stitch.

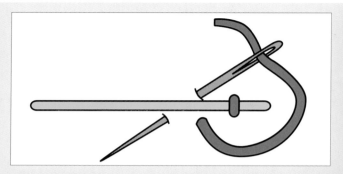

Couching diagram.

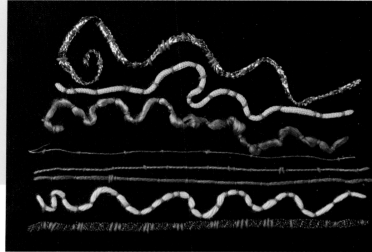

Various decorative threads couched down on a black background.

Couching on gilded cotton scrim.

Machine-made cords couched down on brown velvet.

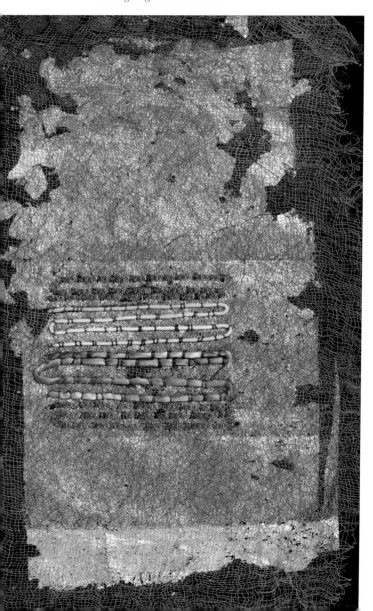

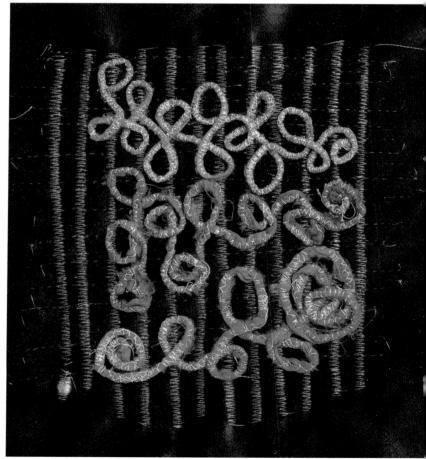

Hand stitched edgings

One aspect of creative textiles is finishing the edges. The following are some tried and tested hand stitched edging techniques. The outcome can be manipulated with the use of different beads, thick or thin threads and overlaying stitch on stitch. All these stitches can be used either on a frayed edge or one that has been turned over. They can be enhanced with beads and in most cases work as a surface stitch as well as an edging stitch. Try using a variegated thread or different colours as you work around your edges.

German stitch

This is also known as German knotted buttonhole stitch. Work two buttonhole stitches slanted apart, then loop the working thread under both without the needle entering the fabric. Then pull the thread downwards.

Step 1

Step 2

A partly beaded German stitch edge.

Antwerp edging stitch

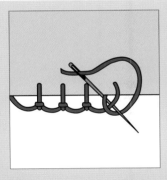

Step 1

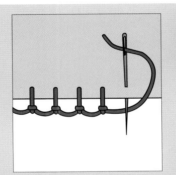

Step 2

An Antwerp edging stitch edge, partly beaded and partly embellished with jump rings.

Eskimo edging stitch

Place the running stitches as evenly as possible a little distance from the edge. Choose the same or a different thread and then wind this through the running stitches both on the back and the front.

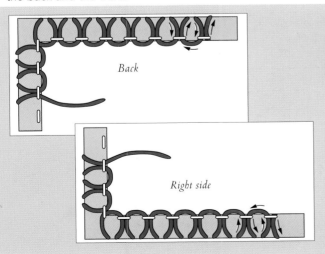

Back

Right side

An Eskimo edging stitch edge. The edge looks the same from the front and back. It can be further enhanced by winding through other threads. Eskimo edging stitch also works well layered over itself, as shown above right in green and yellow.

Machine stitching

One of my constant nags to students is: 'Make sure you read your sewing machine manual!' You should also have your machine serviced at reasonably regular intervals. Invest in a little puffer to remove the fluff and thread ends that inevitably build up from the visible working. If your machine does not perform how it used to, or will not stitch evenly, read the trouble-shooting section in the manual and then seek out a service by someone who has been recommended. Keep some fabric and a pen with your machine and when you start to play with stitches, write the 'recipe' (stitch length, type of thread and pattern) next to the stitch out. It is frustrating trying to replicate an effect when you have no memory of how you formed it.

The threads used for most of the pieces shown is a superior cotton thread with a variegation of colour. Different threads will offer subtly different outcomes. The stitches were made with no alteration to tension unless stated.

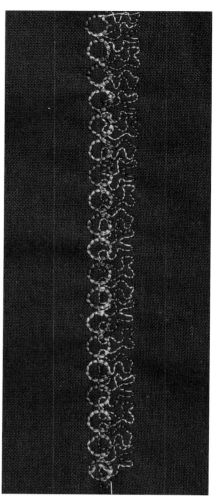

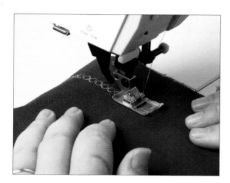

1. Set the machine to a pre-programmed stitch and stitch on to fabric.

2. You can then overlay the first row of stitching by changing to a different pre-programmed stitch and going over the row again.

The finished stitching.

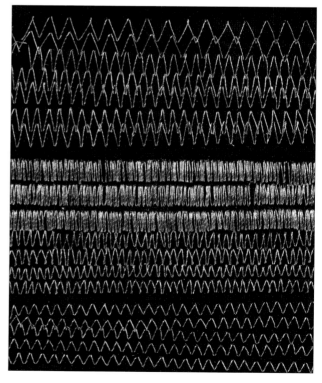

Above: pre-programmed machine stitching in metallic threads on black cotton fabric.
Right: more pre-programmed stitches in metallic threads on black.

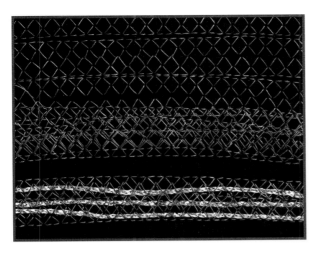

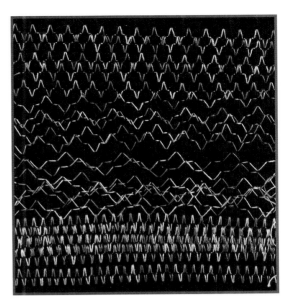

Pre-programmed machine stitching in variegated thread on a black background.

F u r t h e r   i d e a s

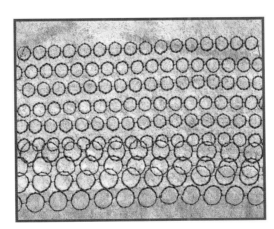

Right: pre-programmed red circles on interlining layered over gold. Far right: pre-programmed machine stitching over metal leaf with sheer fabrics and muslin.

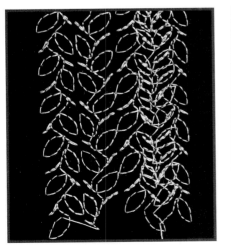

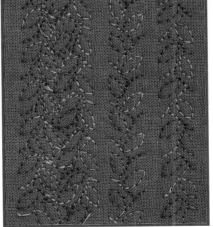

Pre-programmed leaf stitch, white on black (above, left), purple on purple (above, middle), and right: leaf stitch worked over a painted and stamped piece, stitched over and over at the bottom.

Free machining

If you can draw a line with a pencil, then you will be able to free machine. Read your machine manual to locate the knob, button or dial to lower the feed dogs, remove the foot and replace it with either a free machine, free quilting or darning foot. Take the setting to a zero stitch length and a zero stitch width. Some very high end and intelligent machines may resist going all the way to zero but that is fine. You only need to remember a couple of things: the slower you move your fabric, the smaller the stitch. The more you depress the foot pedal, the greater the number of needle hits, and therefore the more stitches will be formed. Quick movement and soft foot pedal pressure will result in bigger stitches, and slow movement with heavy pressure on the foot pedal will lead to small, dense stitching. Some sturdy fabrics will not need any support when sewing in this manner. If your fabric is finer or hard to handle while stitching, or if the stitches cause puckering, you will need to put it into an embroidery hoop to give some integrity/stability to the fabric. For more artful or creative work, you can stabilise the fabric with a sturdy iron-on stabiliser. All the pieces shown had an iron-on stabiliser backing or a piece of craft felt to support the fabric whilst I was stitching in free machine mode.

This shows free machining using a free machine foot. I like to draw the bobbin thread to the top before I start stitching, as it prevents it getting tangled.

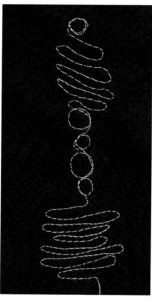

The finished sample.

Gold flake was applied with the glue method (see page 13) with strips of sheer fabric on black fabric. The piece was free machined with a pattern of 'u' shapes.

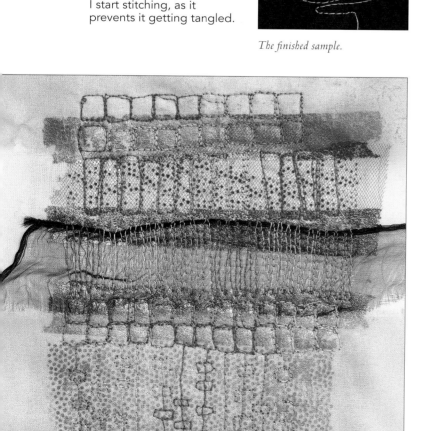

The background was achieved with hot dots, and gold gilding flake applied using a strip of double-sided adhesive sheet. Free machining was then used in a geometric pattern to stitch down layers of sheer fabrics.

The background here is gold gilding flake trapped in interling (see page 10). Using a variety of machine threads, the same pattern was free machined all over in layers and finally the lighter stitching was done with bobbin work (see page 55). The stitch pattern is a rolling scroll.

Further ideas

A painted and stencilled black cotton background with layered free machining. Over-stitching gently distorts the pattern and the fabric to add texture.

This cushion (the other side is shown opposite, top right) was painted randomly with gold and silver coloured fabric paint. The surface was free machined in gold thread. When assembled, the cushion was decorated with a rolled beaded edge (see page 69).

53

Distortion

This approach to free machining offers the possibility of some really exciting three-dimensional stitched structures. The thing to keep in mind when you first have a go at distortion is that you are in control, not the machine! You may have to try a few times to get the rhythm and the flow of how you stitch these pieces but it is well worth the effort. It is still a delight for me whenever I do a distorted piece to see the wriggle and movement that heavy stitching can achieve. Try different blocks of stitching to see how the fabric reacts.

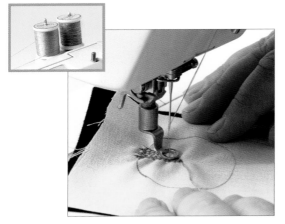

1. Thread up the sewing machine with two top threads and prepare the machine for free machining. Layer cotton fabric on top of felt and draw a circle. Starting in the centre, free machine out to the circle's edge, then go in to the centre again and repeat, stitching tightly spaced radiating lines around the circle.

2. Continue in this way, stitching around the circle. The fabric begins to distort as it is pulled by the dense stitching.

3. When the circle is complete, cut around it with fabric scissors.

Various pieces made using the distortion technique.

Bobbin work

For bobbin work, sometimes known as cable work, the main fabric is backed with felt, and you stitch on to the felt, but the effect you want is created on the reverse (fabric) side. A plain thread is used on the top, and a thicker thread on the bobbin.

1. Unscrew the bobbin with a small screwdriver so that you can loosen the tension to allow for the thicker thread.

2. Wind on the thicker, decorative thread, either by hand, as shown here, or on the machine, following the manufacturer's instructions.

3. Begin stitching in free machine mode (see page 52).

4. As you continue to stitch, you can lift the work to see the effect created on the fabric side, where the bobbin thread shows.

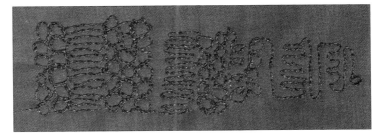

The finished sample.

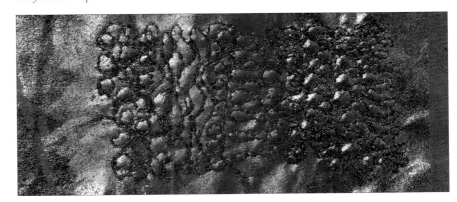

Above: Bobbin work over metal leaf, over-painted.

Left: Bobbin work done with pre-programmed stitches.

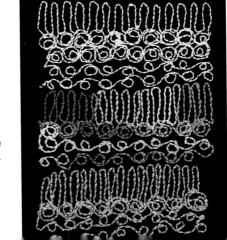

Right: Bobbin work in different lurex threads.

Flower stitcher work

There are videos on the internet showing how the foot works, as when first encountered, it looks rather intimidating, but once you can see the possibilities, it is a must-have item. It works by controlling the movement of the stitch into circles. The variety of patterns that can be achieved is amazing. All the pieces depicted were done on a sewing machine that only had basic stitches such as blind hemming and zigzag. The size of the circle formed is easily manipulated with a sliding bar on the top of the foot, marked with + and – signs. In this way, with a little practice, the circle size can be changed with the work in situ.

Again, I would suggest that notes are kept for patterns that you are likely to want to replicate.

1. Back your fabric with felt. Use a flower stitcher foot with a variegated thread. The foot turns, and stitches a circle of satin stitch (shown here).

2. Change the setting and the flower stitcher stitches a pattern.

3. When your circles are finished, cut them out carefully.

The finished sample.

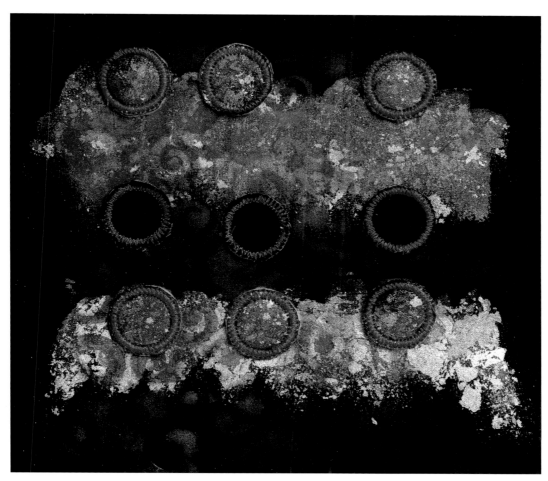

Pieces done with a flower stitcher used on a background decorated with deckle-edged gilding, gilding waxes and fabric paints.

Pieces done with a flower stitcher and then beaded, layered, sequinned and stitched, some with turquoise foiling.

Making cords

These are one of my store cupboard things. They are so useful and if you have a cache of already made cords, you are likely to have one that will fit the bill for your project.

You will need to put an appropriate foot on to your sewing machine: a free machine foot or quilting foot, or indeed some machines have cording feet. I actually prefer a free machine foot. Set your machine to the widest zigzag that will swing over the core you are using, and drop the feed dogs, and you will be able to cover the core as much as you like. It is even possible to use a backwards and forwards movement to create little bobbles.

The yarn or threads used for the cores can be anything from a thin ribbon to string or bundles of thin threads. If a textured yarn is used, the action of the stitch will naturally create a different texture.

When making cords for my store, I use a full bobbin and keep making the cord until that ends. This means I nearly always have enough made up.

You can decorate your own cords using zigzag stitch. Here, silver lurex thread and red cotton threads are being covered with gold metallic thread.

The finished cord.

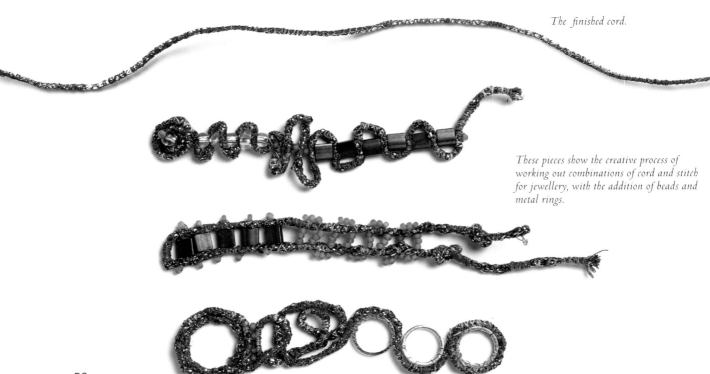

These pieces show the creative process of working out combinations of cord and stitch for jewellery, with the addition of beads and metal rings.

A necklace made with
multiple metallic-thread-
wrapped cords.

This necklace was made
from ring beads wrapped
with cords.

Here, little ring beads have been decorated by
wrapping with cords.

Embellishments

There is something very satisfying about making your own embellishments to create the perfect finishing touch for a project. Here you will learn how to make embellishments from friendly plastic, how to make your own beads, use hooks and eyes for decorative effect and create beaded edges.

What you will need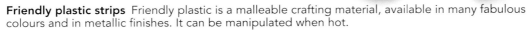

Friendly plastic strips Friendly plastic is a malleable crafting material, available in many fabulous colours and in metallic finishes. It can be manipulated when hot.

Hot craft sheet I have used this to protect my work surface when heating and manipulating friendly plastic.

Craft heat gun This is used to heat friendly plastic.

Cutters These little cutters are like pastry cutters but are specifically for crafts. I have used an angel curve design but you can buy whichever shapes you prefer.

Scissors Good, strong scissors are needed to cut friendly plastic.

Embossing tool A ball-ended tool is used to make the holes in holed bars while the friendly plastic is hot (see page 62).

Silicone cord This is available in a number of different gauges. It is wrapped with friendly plastic to make beads (see page 63).

Rubber stamps Use the grey or red rubber stamping mats, as the clear ones may not be heat resistant.

Silicone moulds These are available for various crafts and are used here with friendly plastic to make embellishments. They are used with **heat-resistant flash** and **heat-resistant spangles** for added sparkle, and with **cotton scrim** so that they can be attached to fabric.
.
Sari yarn This is available from fabric suppliers. I have used a sari yarn 2.5cm (1in) wide for the bead making technique on page 66. You will also need a **long-eyed hand needle**, a second, narrower **yarn**, a **decorative thread**, **seed beads** and **sequins** to make sari yarn beads.

Ring-shaped fashion bead This is used with decorative cord to make the cord-wrapped bead shown on page 66.

Craft wire Malleable, soft coloured wires are needed to make the wire beads shown on page 67, as are seed beads, a **knitting needle**, **pliers** and **wire cutters**.

Hooks and eyes These are used to make decorative chains (see page 68).

Straw or milliner's needle Used for beaded edges. These needles are firm but the eye is flush with the shaft of the needle, so if the bead fits over the pointed end, it will pass over the eye. Use good quality **beads**.

Zip A zip can be used to make a decorative edge for a piece (see page 69).

Using friendly plastic

Friendly plastic has been around since the mid 1970s. It is available in strips of the most scintillating colours, and can easily be manipulated with heat. Although there are several ways of applying heat, I have only used a craft heat tool. However, once you have experienced the adaptability of this material, I would urge you to explore it more widely.

Cutting shapes

1. Cut a piece of friendly plastic large enough to cover an angel curve cutter as shown. Place the piece on a hot craft sheet to protect your work surface.

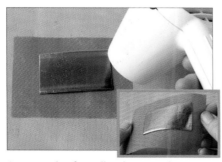

2. Heat the friendly plastic with a heat gun until it is soft. You can tell it is soft by bending the hot craft sheet and seeing whether the friendly plastic bends with it.

3. Press the cutter into the friendly plastic. It should thin the plastic but not cut right through it.

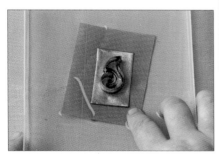

4. Place the piece, on the hot craft sheet, in cold water to cool down.

5. The back of the friendly plastic shows the shape of the angel curve cutter just breaking the surface. Pull the cutter away from the friendly plastic to separate the shape from the void.

6. Push the shape out of the angel curve cutter using a tool if necessary.

Friendly plastic flowers used on a finished piece. These were also made using a cutter.

The angel curve shape and its void. Both can be used in projects.

Holed bars

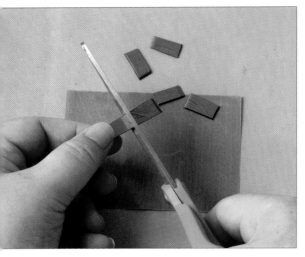

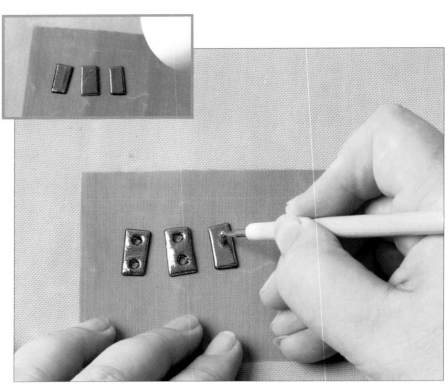

1. Cut rectangles of friendly plastic on to a hot craft sheet.

2. Heat the bars with the heat gun until they are soft. Use a ball tool to make holes in the bars. Place the hot craft sheet and bars in cold water to cool.

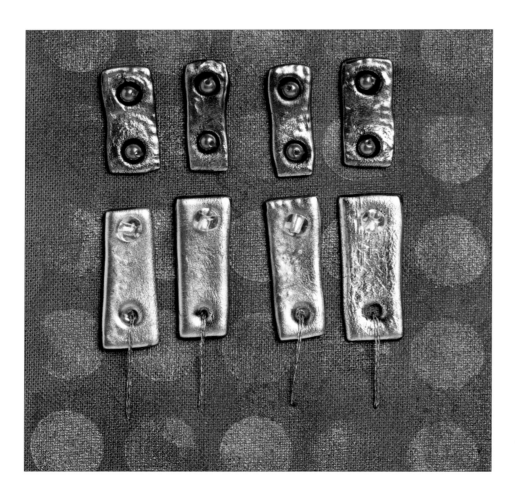

A finished piece featuring holed bars, beads and stitches on painted fabric.

Making beads

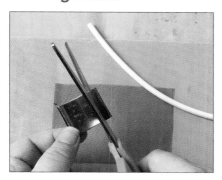

1. Cut friendly plastic to the width you require, and long enough to wrap round a silicone cord.

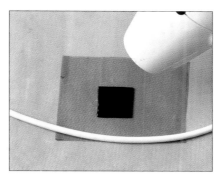

2. Place it face down and heat it with a heat gun until soft.

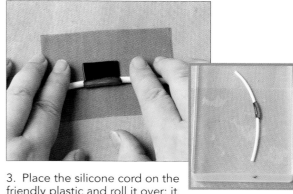

3. Place the silicone cord on the friendly plastic and roll it over; it will pick up the plastic. Drop the cord and plastic straight into cold water.

4. For the next layer of the bead, cut a contrasting piece of friendly plastic that is narrower than the first, to leave a border.

5. Heat the new piece of friendly plastic and roll the cord and the original bead over it, so that it is rolled up in the middle of the first layer. Drop the cord and bead straight into water again to cool it.

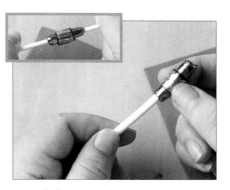

6. Pull the ends of the silicone cord to stretch it. This helps to release the bead. Slide the bead off the end.

Finished friendly plastic beads.

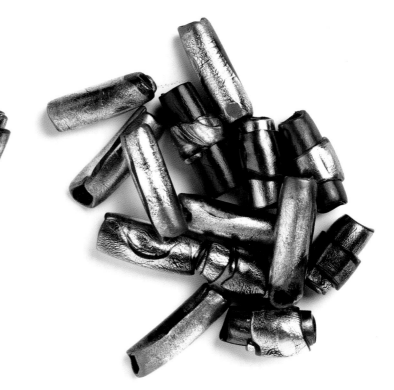

Stamping

1. Cut a piece of friendly plastic and heat it with the heat gun on a hot craft sheet. While it is soft, stamp it with a large rubber stamp.

2. Place the stamp, friendly plastic and hot craft sheet together in cold water to cool.

3. When it is cool, remove the friendly plastic from the stamp.

The stamped friendly plastic.

Moulding

Adding cotton scrim to friendly plastic enables the moulded element to be stitched to a background. Any excess material can be trimmed. Use cotton scrim in a colour sympathetic to the background.

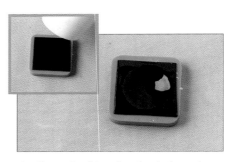

1. Cut a piece of friendly plastic to fit a circular mould.

2. Sprinkle heat resistant flash and heat resistant spangles into the mould.

3. Place the friendly plastic face down on top of the mould and heat it with the heat gun until it slumps into the mould as shown.

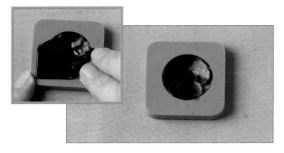

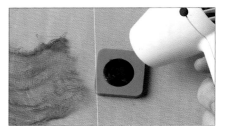

4. Put moisturiser on your fingers to prevent the friendly plastic from sticking, and fold the edges of the friendly plastic into the mould to make a neat circle.

5. Allow the friendly plastic to cool in the mould, or put the mould into cold water. Pull the mould away from the piece.

6. Have a piece of scrim ready. Put the cool piece back into the mould and use the heat gun for a moment to heat the flat surface only.

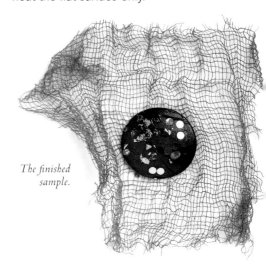

7. Press the scrim into the melted flat surface of the piece to attach it.

8. When it is cool, take the piece out of the mould.

The finished sample.

Moulded friendly plastic pieces.

Further ideas

A moulded friendly plastic piece with scrim
attached, on a gilded background.

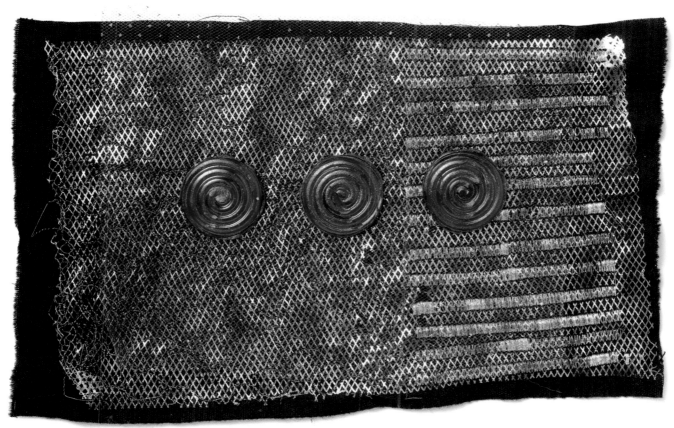

Moulded friendly plastic pieces on a piece foiled with gossamer webbing and stitched.

Beads and bits

Sari yarn beads

1. Take a ball of sari yarn and roll up the end to make a little ball. Wind the yarn round one way then change direction slightly and carry on winding. When you have the size of ball you want, cut the yarn.

2. Introduce another yarn by wrapping the end over the end of the sari yarn and holding it in place. Wrap the sari yarn bead to decorate it, then cut the end of the second yarn.

3. Thread a long-eyed needle with decorative thread. Tuck the end of the second yarn under the wrapped yarn and stab stitch through it, and through the whole bead. Continue stab stitching randomly through the bead both to hold it together and to decorate it. Snip off the thread at the end.

The finished sari yarn bead.

Various sari yarn beads, some decorated with beads and sequins.

Cord-wrapped beads

1. Take a ring-shaped fashion bead and wrap cord around the ring, without cutting the cord from the ball.

2. Wrap the ring as widely or as closely as you like, and when you are pleased with it, cut off the end of the cord, leaving a length as shown.

3. Wrap the final length round until it is on top of the other end. Thread a needle with matching thread and stitch through the two cord ends a few times to secure. Trim the ends of the cord to finish.

The finished cord-wrapped bead.

Wire beads

1. Thread beads directly on to a spool of wire.

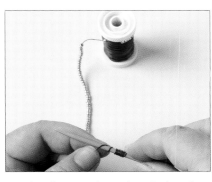

2. Closely wrap the unbeaded end of the wire round a knitting needle to create the core of the bead.

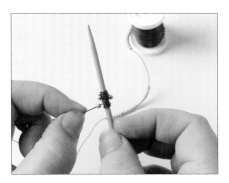

3. Push a bead along to the wrapped core, wrap the wire around the knitting needle, then push another bead along, and continue.

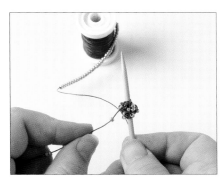

4. Carry on pushing beads along and wrapping wire until you have the size and shape of bead that you want.

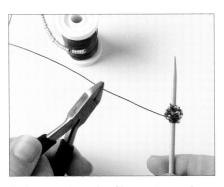

5. Leave a length of bare wire at the end, and cut with wire cutters.

6. Use flat-nosed pliers to twist the end of the wire through one of the decorative beads. Then twist and push the wire end into the body of the wire bead to finish.

Various wire beads.

Hooks and eyes

1. Attach the hook to the eye and crush to secure using flat-nosed pliers.

2. Use two sets of pliers to open a split ring.

3. Take the original hook and eye and thread one of the loops of the eye on to the split ring. Take another hook and thread one of its loops on to the same split ring. Close the split ring using pliers.

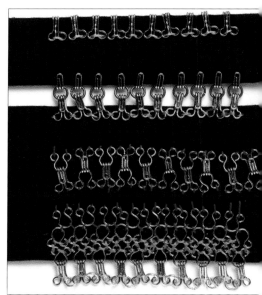

4. Take another split ring and thread on the other loops of the eye and the new hook as shown. You can continue in this way to make the length of chain you require.

These hook and eye chains have been coloured using solvent markers.

Hooks and eyes have been used here with coloured stitching, both to decorate a piece and to attach one panel to another.

Beaded edges

Beading the edges of my work has been part of my signature for a long time. Shown here are a few of the simple but very decorative edges that I like. Beads offer the possibility of adding colour and shape to edges. Use a good thread and a straw or milliner's needle. Always use good beads – cheap irregular ones can be deeply frustrating when sewing them on because of size inconsistencies. The bead size you use is a personal choice, but I recommend not using very heavy beads for edge work as they will pull and potentially distort your piece.

A single beaded edge

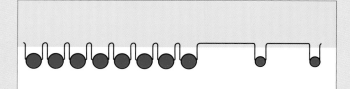

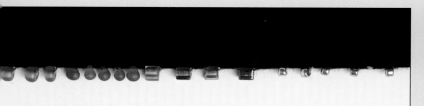

A looped beaded edge

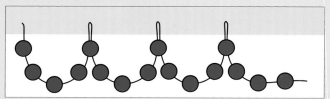

A triangular beaded edge

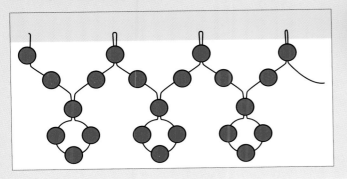

A rolled beaded edge

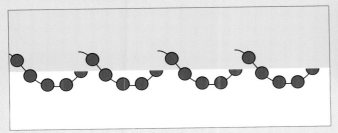
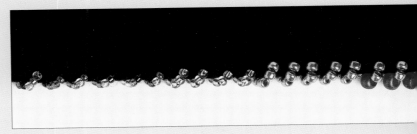

A brick stitch edge

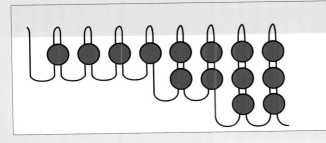
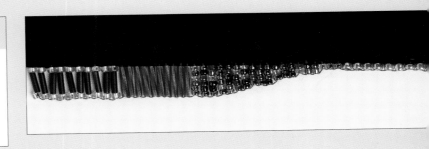

A zip edge

Using the decorative qualities of a zip can be very useful. If you use a metal-toothed zip, it can be coloured and the fabric can add stability to a soft or cut edge. The zip can be stitched decoratively or in an understated way.

Here, fly stitch was used to attach the zip edge to brown paper fabric.

Jewellery
Creations

Sometimes it is just nice to be able to wear your art! Some necklaces can be as time-consuming as major artworks, but they are well worth the effort. If you don't wear necklaces, try a bracelet or brooch.

Clockwise from top: bronze, copper and green friendly plastic beads with wrapped cord knotting; green and mauve friendly plastic beads with wrapped cord knotting and a hook and eye chain; cord-wrapped wooden beads, laced with wrapped cords and ribbons; green sari yarn beads threaded with toning shiny green beads; domed felt-backed metal circles (see page 30) stitched together with hook and eye links coloured to match with solvent markers.

The central piece is made from painted and printed fabric similar to that on page 43 (bottom row). The circles were cut out, stitched together and lightly padded, then beaded and attached to each other with press studs and beaded chains.

Moulds, Sparkle and Stitch

This detail shows the Eskimo edging stitch edge (see page 49), the moulded friendly plastic circle and the foiled background.

The background was foiled using fusible web as shown on page 21. I then took a very openly woven dyed cotton scrim. Numerous friendly plastic mouldings were made, with heat-resistant jewels added prior to casting for extra sparkle. The mouldings were attached to the scrim using the method described on page 64. The whole piece was hand stitched with running stitches and edged with Eskimo edging stitch. Beads were then individually stitched around the friendly plastic shapes both to secure them and to enlarge the circular forms.

Copper Shimmer, Green Glow

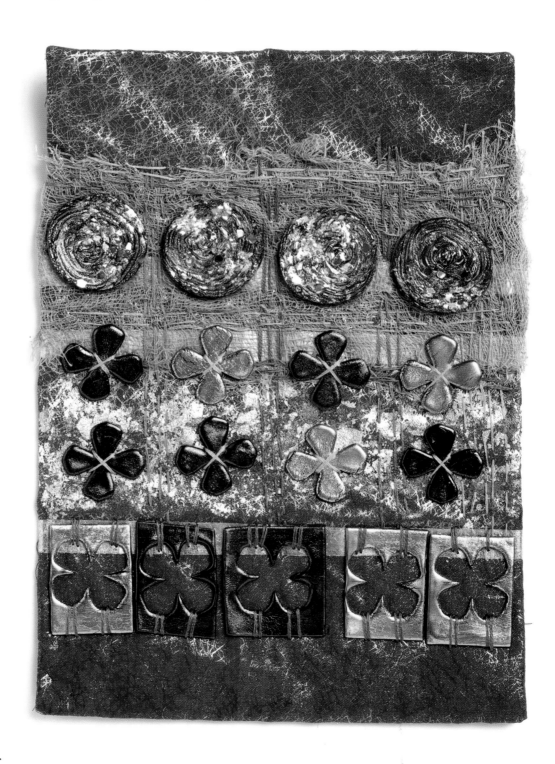

The background was made using gossammer webbing (see page 22) with a rich terracotta cotton base fabric. Friendly plastic shapes were moulded, as shown on page 64, and flower shapes were cut out as shown on page 61. Before the piece was assembled, an area of deckle-edged gilding was added (see page 13). The individual elements were assembled, and hand stitching was used both to secure elements and to decorate the piece. The edges were simply folded over.

This detail shows the foiled background and the running stitch used to decorate this piece. Friendly plastic in two shades of green was cut with a flower cutter, and both the flower shapes and the voids have been used in the design.

Circles, Rubies and Shine

Not quite rubies, but little glass and sequin elements add that ruby glow to this layered piece. It features flower stitcher circles (see page 56) with Antwerp edging stitch edges (see page 49) and added beads. The background was layered over fusible web with gold gilding flake, sheer fabrics, glossy netting and dyed cotton scrim. All the elements were stitched in place and the piece was decorated with running stitch. The edges of the piece were finished with German stitch (see page 49).

The detail shows the running stitch decoration, the German stitch edging and the flower stitcher circles with beaded edges.

Paper, Circles and Beads

The background was made
using brown paper fabric
(see page 9). The surface
embellishments include cords
which were made as shown
on page 58, then couched
down on to the surface (see
page 48), and die-cut circular
elements with flower stitcher
centres. These elements were
further embellished with
beaded accents. Handmade wire
beads (see page 67) adorn the
scalloped bottom edge.

*This detail shows the brown paper fabric
background and the use of cords, decorations
made with a flower stitcher and wire beads.*

Beads, Zips, Hooks and Eyes

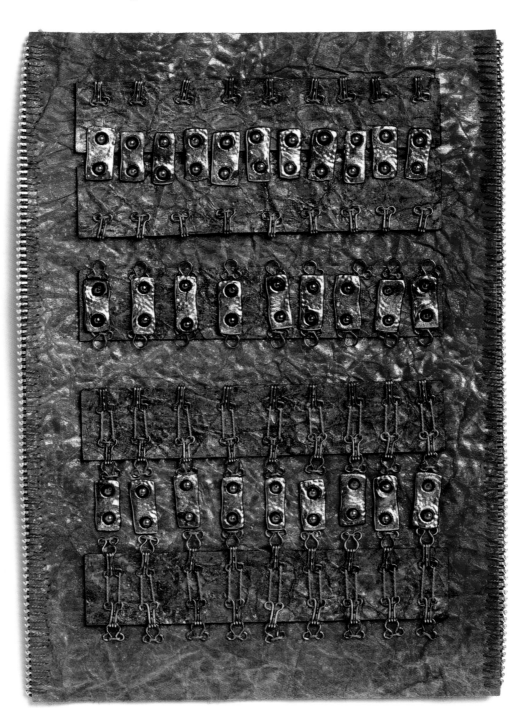

The background is brown paper fabric (see page 9). The edge was then supported with a zip (see page 69) and stitched down between each tooth to further decorate the edge. Small holed bars were made from friendly plastic (see page 62). Strips of brown paper fabric were cut and trapped down with alcohol ink-coloured hooks and eyes, and the holed bars stitched in place with a bead in each hole.

This detail shows the holed bars in friendly plastic, the hooks and eyes and the zip edge.

Turquoise Treasure

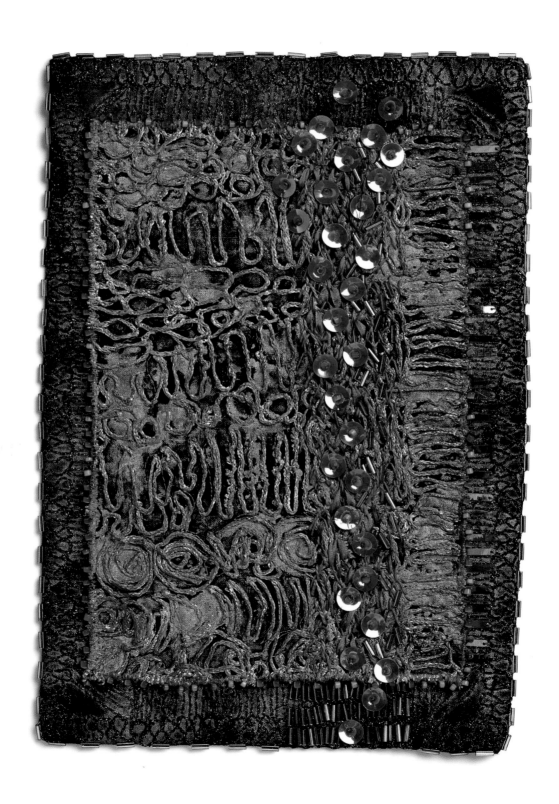

For this piece, two pieces of
black cotton fabric were dabbed
with paint. Each piece was then
stitched freely with bobbin work
(see page 55), concentrating
on the outer edge on one of
the black pieces and the inner
area on the other. The stitch
was then over-painted to give a
richer presentation of colour.
The inner panel was cut to fit
the centre of the other piece.
Further stitching, including
many layers of fly stitch (see
page 46) was added, and then

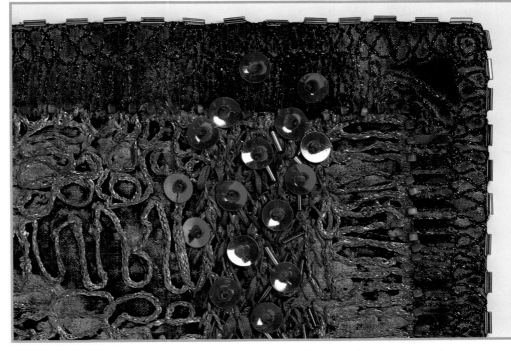

matching sequins were placed over this (now quite deep) area of stitch.
The edge of the supporting panel was then folded over and stitched
with a single beaded edge (see page 68). The bugle beads used hug the
edge and just give a glint of extra colour.

*This detail shows painted fabric, over-painted
bobbin work, layered fly stitch, sequins and
beaded edges on both the inner and outer panels.*

Purple Panels, Beaded Bowls

The large supporting panel was made using gossamer webbing, as shown on page 22. This was then thoroughly over-stitched with a Greek key style pre-programmed stitch (see page 50). Additional detailing was added with lock stitch (see page 47). The main panel was decorated with deckle-edged gilding (see page 13) and using double-sided adhesive sheet (page 14). The panel was then stitched and over-stitched with lock stitch.

Separate stitched circles were created using the distortion method shown on page 54. The stitch direction was round and round so that instead of a wave form, little bowl shapes were created. These were further beaded. The piece was assembled and sequins added, as well as a single beaded edge (see page 68).

This detail shows the deckle-edged gilding, foiling, craft stickers, a beaded distorted circle, the lock stitch decoration and the beaded edge on the main panels.

Shimmering
Vessels

To make these vessels, a large piece of fabric was painted and printed using fabric painting techniques shown on pages 40–41, including using dense foam stamps, using stencils, rubber stamping and lifting off paint.

A simple pattern was cut out for the vessels and the section was backed with craft felt. The edges were then

stitched with Antwerp edging stitch (see page 49). This stitch is very versatile as it can be interlaced to join sections together, and beads can also be added. When the main vessel was complete, domed metal circles were added for decoration (see page 30).

Peacock Panel

This shimmering turquoise piece with its cicular elements has the eye-catching appeal of a peacock's tail. The background has a mixture of deckle-edged gilding (see page13) and fusible web as shown on page 21. The decorative circles feature machine embossed metal rings (see page 28), pierced and stitched on to black felt circles, with beads sewn on in each pierced hole. German stitch (see page 49) was used to finish the edges neatly, and parts of the edge were also beaded. Metal embellishments were rubbed with gilding wax and stitched on, with beads in the centres.

This detail shows the use of three embellishments rubbed with gilding wax, and the beaded edge.

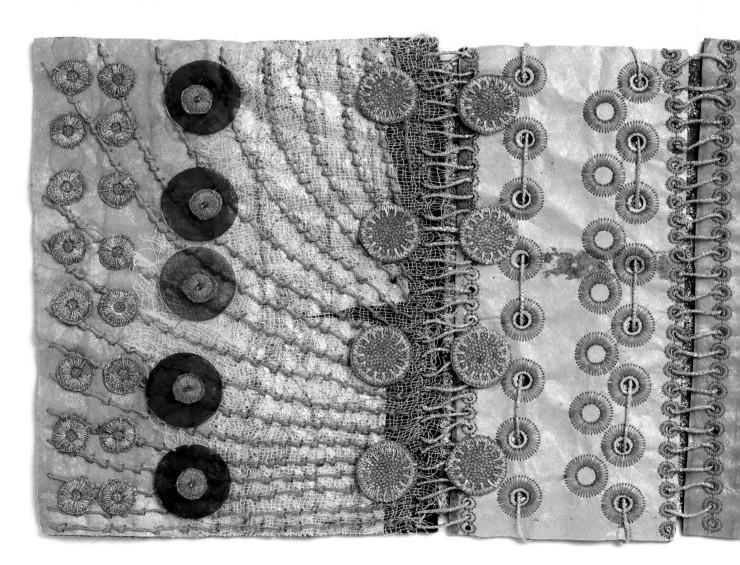

Stitched Panels, Mica Shine

The background panels for this piece were made by layering interlining with metal leaf (see page 10). Two of the panels are decorated with mica circles coloured with alcohol inks (see page 33), following the rich, orangey tones of the fabric. Keeping the circle theme running throughout, the panels were laced with machine cords, and the eyelets were done using a pre-programmed feature of one of my machines – but you could use metal eyelets. Flower stitcher circles were also used (see page 56), some beaded and some decorated with hot dots, (see page 24). Coral stitch in sweeping curves decorates the left-hand panel (see page 47).

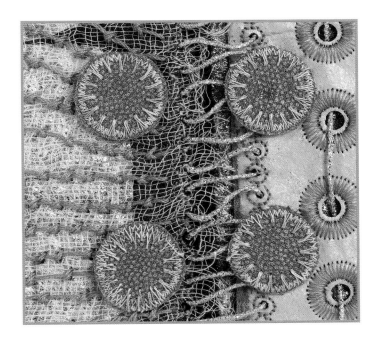

This detail shows the use of coral stitch and mica circles decorated with flower stitcher circles.

This detail shows the way the panels are laced together using cords, and circles decorated with hot dots.

Shimmering Silver, Domed Delight

For the background to this piece, black cotton fabric was decorated with deckle-edged gilding (see page 13), and with stencilling using a glue stick and gilding flake (page 16). This was over-painted with pearlescent fabric paints using the same circles stencil. Sculptural elements were created by doming circles of silver metal (see page 30) and using the distortion method (see page 54) on black felt circles with stitching in lime green, turquoise and purple.

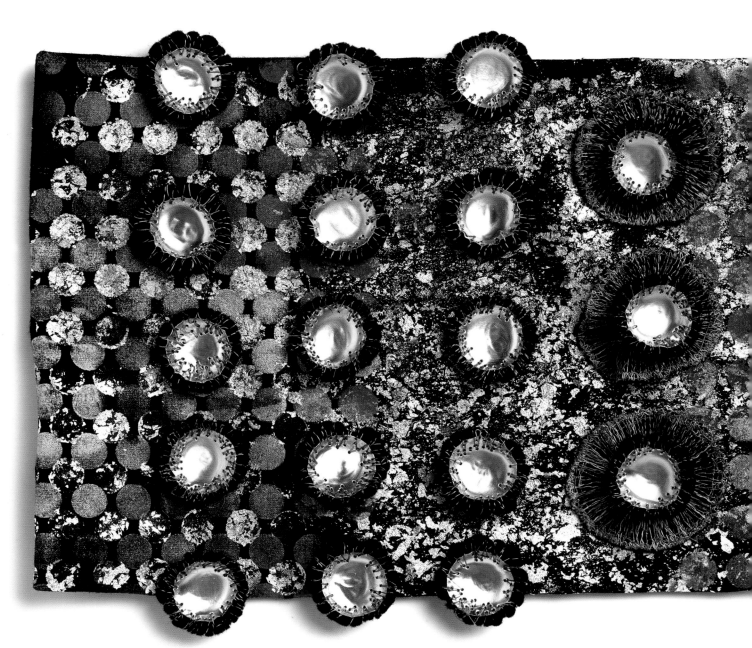

This detail shows domed circles, and a distorted circle with a domed circle in the centre.

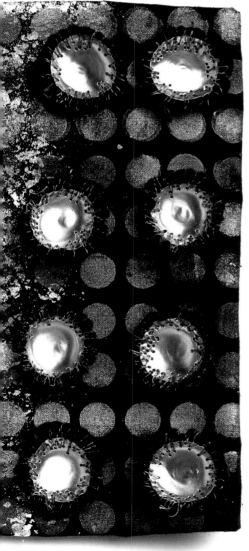

Stitched, Shining Beaded Bag

The fabric pieces for this bag were created by layering pieces of black fabric with gilding flake, interlining and sheer fabrics (see pages 10–11). One of the fabric pieces was then decorated with free machining (see page 52) in toning colours; the other with pre-programmed machine stitching (page 50). To make the main body of the bag, two rectangles were cut from these prepared pieces to suit the metal bag handles. One of the rectangles was further embellished with hand stitching. The bag was assembled from the two rectangles using the instructions that accompanied the bag handles. It was lined with a blue spotted fabric. The edges were stitched and beaded, and feature beads made using the sari yarn method shown on page 66 were attached at the bottom to complete the rich, sumptuous look of this bag.

The other side of the bag.